Elegy for Virginia Redding

William Lane

Mad River Press

ISBN 0-944156-01-0
First Edition

A few of these poems first appeared in
Hanging Loose and *Journal of New Jersey Poets*

Mad River Press
State Road
Richmond, Mass. 01254

To all those who labor in small towns for peace

The Goats at Dusk

At dusk there is
silence in the little, three-sided barn;
light in the cracks between the boards
is pink and grey.
The open side faces the full moon,
staring through trees.
I watch the goats eating
their pale green alfalfa.
Beards of alfalfa sprout
from their mouths, the pupils of their eyes
are dark rectangles.

Like zany mystics
they eat grass
and live in a world
where not one thing is named.

Us

Perhaps time will empty us, poor citizens.
Time emptied saint
after saint
kneeling on stone steps of History,
leaving only light
within their faintly trembling heads—
but us?
Distorted by our jobs,
the clothes we must wear,
the life of our nation?

We weep
in the chapel
of the laundromat,
in the cathedral of the workplace;
our loves,
our revolutions,
impacted like teeth.

Wishes in the Year of the Pig

We stand
in your kitchen
full coffee cups steaming in sunlight.
Your young son walks
the boundary between us,
clicking his heels,
eyeing us
poor flesh that we are,
Reaganized
all year by talk of war,
oppressed by glittering, jewel-laden schemes
of the president
and O the summer flies that buzz
already bearing our hope away
drop by drop, I'd swear
we're all boundary walkers
in this bad season
for love
and justice!
May your son be strong
in the days that will come!
May words serve him
gathering like moths at the screen!
May colors live under his fingertips!
May others live in him, and he in others!
May all creatures
live a second time
in his heart
when he sings!

Salamander

Lifted from beneath wet, rotted bark
in cold October,
a sleek, small god
bearing the clownish burden

of yellow spots on a green body
quieted now by the season of smoke
rising steadily like prayer from lawns;
and the glass of his eyes

set beneath a wide forehead,
dark blue as night one hour old
through which an ambulance glides
on rain slick streets

its lights turning in silence.

Mozote

"She said that it was on the evening of December 11 that troops of the Atlacatl Brigade had come to Mozote. The Brigade is an elite, 1,000-man unit of the Salvadoran Army, well known at least by name to most Salvadorans, that has been trained for rapid deployment and anti-guerilla offensives by U. S. advisors here."

Washington Post, January 27, 1982

Money moves southward across the Caribbean
more silently than the opening of a hand.
Money hangs in the air above the tile roofs of the villages,
shimmering like heat.

And in the accompanying photograph
a radio crackles. Soldiers raise empty eyes
toward a passing helicopter.
A body smolders in a ditch
beside the ruins of the whitewashed chapel.
Within the rectangle of broken down walls
bones smolder. A soldier, with a long stick,
stirs the bones.

Once upon a time
the rich came planting money seeds
where food used to grow
and now the gum chewing Atlacatl Brigade
is money in full bloom.

The Weight of Stone

The weight
of stone is
peace
for hands that know
the weightlessness of words.
Four bearded boys,
dreamers wise
to what can
be told
and portable in
weightless lines,
we sigh in the glittering April wind
and curve like dancers
over the mossy
flesh of rock,
lifting with bent, trembling legs
this squarish body
heavy as half
a car.
It comes alive
only when we strain
upward
marveling
at the weakness
of our plans.

Struck with a hammer
it gives off
the bitter smell of time.
I love the strength of its stillness.
Its patience would be
ecstasy
in a living
thing.
Our touch so light,
our hands weak as kisses
on its dreamless forehead,
it holds us here
straining upward,
empty-headed and glad of it
in the April sun.

History Lesson

Always remember how in those difficult times
objects acquired voices while men and women fell silent.
Stones developed personalities
and sank to the bottom of streams.
Even brooms were found to be leading secret lives
but the human heart stood clear as glass
and the poor soul not even knowing its right name
hovered above its product chattering like a loose gear
while salamandrous evangelicals
made big money telling lies about God,
and the poets, mirroring the age,
grew lumpish and querulous, while in their poems
a thousand doves returning from the future crackled like radios,
and the bedrooms of the rich, adorned in blinking lights,
spun slowly on their towers.

Driving to Work

You know those heroic autumn days,
sky still wine dark, crypto-homeric,
and you drive to work
passing barns lit from within
and houses still darkened,
and the poplars and oaks, pole straight,
colonnading in the ghost light;
trees, it seems, turned inside out for autumn,
we drive to work
blank as the steadily brightening, cloudless sky:

For the spirit of the lucky one
is like a barn lit from within
when the whole life of another
is like a darkened house,
and desires are hard as coins
when driving is a kind of waiting
and work, only a kind of waiting;
and the simple truth about us,
if it escaped our flesh,
would burn cold and separate
as a newly risen sun.

Shadow Project

They are
dead whiteness
you could scrape
with a knife
and gather
into a sticky handful.
Their bodies are thin as one coat of paint!
Yet when they lie down
upon the pavements of empire
they are language
fingertips can read,
flesh understand.
Shape by shape,
letter by letter
they go down
under the rumble of trucks,
under the hurry of shined shoes,
under the bare, translating toes
of silent curious children:

Yes, let the children read
with the soles of their naked feet
and be whole someday at last!

Elegy for Virginia Redding

community activist d. 1982

Wise woman I suppose
in the end you chose
the death you were given
letting regrets fall like blossoms
fluttering down petal by petal from the tree,
their moment gone, their glory spent,
but crossing the tracks in my wide old car
near the packing house heading home
from one more meeting, one more event,
I see our losses breaking like Atlantic waves
on a far shore.
And in the mindless drumming of rain on the roof
I think I hear ten winters make a single night
where we drive around looking for meetings, you and I,
and shyly, shyly you hold my hand
as we pause in the road for deer to cross
and marvel at their grace, their lifted heads,

their dazzling, inhuman eyes.

*

Catholic farm wife,
mother of 15:
Words came hard
for you
at first
they were delicate, elusive creatures
shining like the bubbles
a child
at your elbow
was continually blowing
as we talked in the street
one sunny afternoon
of the Vietnam era
looking for the right words
while delicate bubbles
drifted all around us:

*

The shiny, steel, engraved comb
made from a bit of jet bomber wing
a Mennonite brought us to hold one night
while he spoke on the war,
do you remember?
And the handbag
woven of many colored wire
from torn up jungle surveillance systems,
both passed round our circle of twelve or so one night
late in the war while the Mennonite spoke:

A quarter inch thick almost, cut from a downed B-52
that comb in our hands
was like a word,
and the colorful handbag
a second, woven word
in a language
we were slowly learning:

We the world famous, North American middle classes,
floating upon empire
like ducks on a farm pond
as we lived

our lives.

*

On May 1, 1983, one year
and two months after your death,
in the inner courtyard of the main hospital
in Managua, Nicaragua,
Tomás Borge,
Minister of Interior,
speaks softly,
shakes the hands
of the American visitors, friends
of Nicaragua,
as the coffins of those killed
the day before by the contras
are carried past us.

13 coffins move slowly
through the crowd,
some loaded
with flowers.
In the crowded hallway
we press against the wall
but flowers brush our faces
as the dead pass by.
I breathe
uneasily
and see that even here ten feet away

someone is reading a newspaper.
On the front page
under a banner headline
one of the dead, a West German doctor,
young and handsome in the family snapshot,

smiles enigmatically.

*

Six weeks of sickness and you in bed,
your will like a spider's thread
glittering in sunlight.
Shadows of clouds hurry across the land
all day.
Your daughters comb your hair and sing
while you watch the light hanging in the windows:
They are creatures, they are blossoms
along a common branch, full of unknowing.
But O the stillness when they rest, arm in arm.

*

Your coffin I carried
one end of
above a sluggish, brown creek
on a green hill
in earliest spring:

Such light leavings, Virginia,
after so much passionate
patience, so much life!
A body lighter than a mustard seed
entrusted to six sets of hands,
six sober gentlemen
dressed in their best dark suits
to please death.

It was death's day.
Three boys had
to be chased out of
your waiting grave
by the sweating
funeral director
and I remember
the sides of the grave
sliced clean as birthday cake
and little girls

in silk dresses
with armloads of flowers
passing among the crowd.

Death was pleased.

*

Spring will come again, Virginia.
The dead once again
will give themselves
to the land.
The apple trees will fill
with blossoms.
And I will photograph a tractor driver
dismounted for a moment beside a tree,
the one with the scar across his middle
like a sentence in Hebrew
hidden now beneath a heavy, green workshirt;
a slender, sunburned, quiet man,
and a steady pain at the bottom of his throat
which only shows in one shoulder's half stoop

and a grey cap the brim turned slightly to one side
standing among the heavily laden, flowering branches.
In the photograph
his face is calm
serving death
which has broken into blossom
all around him.

*

They say
the best are seeds,
make themselves seeds
through years of struggle
adding their small strength to the earth's
when they die,
coming back in dreams
drops of water glistening in their hair,
their voices shimmering in the air
like heat, telling it all at last,
adding their strength to ours
one dream at a time.
And so you, too, Virginia,

come back
one word, one act, one meeting at a time,

and your truth is like
a square of winter sunlight
on the floor
in which my cat camps.

*

We drive to the peace march, Virginia.
Then walk beneath the sparkling white dome
of the capitol,
what light, we say
to one another,
under a cloudless blue sky,
what Egyptian vibrations
are here among the stark white buildings of democracy
reflected in gigantic pools.

We who thinking to survive
had made ourselves so small
now crying out in protest
return again to normal size
at least in imagination

at least for today
walking these governmental streets
reflecting upon the strength
of a dead woman;

for the strength of such a woman
is compact and articulate as a fist,
is sunlight falling between the buildings into the streets,
is a song passed from hoarse voice
to hoarse voice in a moving crowd:

And when the march slows to a stop
and people start clapping, Virginia,
a woman is dancing, really dancing,
in a circle the crowd moves back to form,
and her baby rides,
her baby rides in the glory seat of her palm.